JOYCE'S DUBLIN

FIRST PUBLISHED IN GREAT BRITAIN IN 2000 BY CAXTON EDITIONS
AN IMPRINT OF CAXTON PUBLISHING GROUP
20 BLOOMSBURY STREET, LONDON WC1 3QA

ISBN 1-84067-149-1

A COPY OF THE CIP DATA IS AVAILABLE FROM THE
BRITISH LIBRARY UPON REQUEST.

ART DIRECTED, DESIGNED AND PRODUCED FOR CAXTON EDITIONS
BY KEITH POINTING DESIGN CONSULTANCY.

REPROGRAPHICS BY GA GRAPHICS
PRINTED AND BOUND IN
SINGAPORE BY STAR STANDARD

ACKNOWLEDGMENTS
THE IRISH TOURIST BOARD
FOR THE SUPPLY OF PHOTOGRAPHS

FOR LAUREN

JOYCE'S DUBLIN
AN ILLUSTRATED COMMENTARY

ROSANNA NEGROTTI

CAXTON EDITIONS

I've been to Paradise but I've never been to me.

Charlene

CONTENTS

1

IN DUBLIN'S FAIR CITY

DEAD BLACK through the aeroplane window, looking down over the Irish Sea on a cloudless night. Then clusters of orange lights, quickly focusing into the city of Dublin, getting larger as the plane descends. My first view of the city is dark and abstract, made up of pinpricks of brightness. James Joyce – whose writing was an ongoing process of plotting the city out – I wonder if he would recognise its outline, this illuminated skeleton of Dublin from the sky.

There's a statue of James Joyce in Dublin. A middle-aged, bespectacled Joyce, standing on Talbot Street in bronze. He leans on a walking stick, resting. He could be mid-stroll, peering about. Up the road Olhausen's shop

Statue of Joyce in St Stephen's Green

still stands, the butcher's in *Ulysses* where Leopold Bloom goes to buy sausages. Dublin past and present: Dublin in a work of fiction. The city is almost a character in itself in Joyce's work: all his novels and stories refer back to it, introducing its streets, shops, landmarks. Dublin is used as both backdrop and reference point: it's a locale through which his protagonists can move, plotted carefully, often road by road.

At this moment, Dublin is a changing place. London's Evening Standard describes it as the ideal place for a weekend shopping trip. Money from Brussels has been pumped into the city, and for the first time in 150 years, emigration is in the opposite direction. The American-Irish are actually being invited back from the United States, and there's a surplus of jobs, particularly in the building trade. Building sites are scattered across the city, revamping dereliction to create spaces for sushi and cappuccino. A kind of consumer sophistication is being brought to the place, like a smaller, brighter

Dublin is full of character

Joyce left Dublin in 1904 at the age of 22, in a kind of voluntary exile. He lived in Europe for the rest of his life, with a only a few short trips back. Yet Dublin remained the backbone to his fiction, as did its citizens. He used the city as a kind of stage, peopling it with those he knew, often renamed. Joyce's friend Vincent Cosgrave recognised himself in *A Portrait of the Artist as a Young Man*, and remonstrated with Joyce as to why he was named Lynch (a notorious judge from Galway, who hanged his own son for murder in 1493). And in *Ulysses* Leopold Bloom lives at 7 Eccles Street – in real life the home of JF Byrne, another of Joyce's friends. It's curious that Joyce should make one of his characters live at his friend's house. Why that exact address, given the million possible homes in the city? Byrne even resurfaces in *Portrait* but this time named Cranley, so that the connections become even more complex. It's debatable whether Joyce ever created a single character from nowhere: everyone seems to be a stylised form of somebody else, each protagonist seems to grow from an accumulation of associated memories.

The Bank of Ireland

Streets, people, places. A way for the exile, remembering, to stay close to home. And it's all still here somewhere, though as time passes, things are increasingly buried, knocked down along with the decaying buildings. Number 7 Eccles Street was demolished in 1982, to build a hospital. Some things, quite rightly, are more important than literary fictions. The people Joyce knew are all dead now, though their descendants probably remain, scattered round the city. Most will be unaware that their ancestors pop up in *Ulysses* or *Portrait* or *Finnegans Wake*. And those who do know were those closest to Joyce, maybe even a bit peeved about their literary representation at the time. Even the librarian at the National Library of Ireland was taken by surprise. Long after Joyce's death in 1941, Richard Best was approached by the

I'm still standing: John Mulligan's bar on Poolbeg Street

BBC for an interview. 'What makes you come to me?' he said. 'What makes you think I have any connection with this man Joyce?' 'You can't deny the connection' said the BBC representative, 'You're a character in *Ulysses*.' 'I am not a character in fiction,' replied Dr Best. 'I am a living being.'

It's hard with Joyce to differentiate life from fable. Molly Bloom in *Ulysses* has elements of Nora Barnacle, the woman Joyce spent his life with (though Nora did try to distance herself from the character, stating flatly that Molly was fatter). Whilst Stephen Dedalus (in both *Ulysses* and *Portrait*) is a reworking of Joyce himself, more or less. Yet there's a lot of scope for ambiguity in 'more or less'. What's missing, what's included. Joyce was paranoid that Nora was unfaithful (she wasn't); Molly Bloom has afternoon sex with Blazes Boylan, whilst her husband Leopold is out. And Oliver St John Gogarty, Joyce's one-time friend. Joyce transformed him into Buck Mulligan, the grandiloquent intellectual lout who opens *Ulysses* at the Martello Tower. Joyce stayed at the tower with Gogarty for a short period in

Mosaic outside a Dublin pub

1904, so that the very first words of *Ulysses* are both storytelling and real life. It is difficult to separate out all the different strands: to mark the point where biography ends and fiction begins.

When I leave my hotel on Parnell Square on my first morning in Dublin, Oliver St John Gogarty's house is at number 5, marked by a brown, oval plaque. It's slightly down-at-heel these days, its door painted in matt blue, with dusty panels. It's a dark day and the lights are off, so nobody is at home. I don't think it's anybody's office, and I like the fact that this grand residence is still used for domestic purposes. A lantern still stands by the front door, at the top of three small steps. So this is where the model for Buck Mulligan lived, the character who opens *Ulysses*. I'm thrilled that I've only to trip out the door, and here is the first clue, my first small landmark in the unveiling of Joyce's Dublin.

Model character? Oliver St John Gogarty (1878-1957), the medical student Joyce transformed into Buck Mulligan

2

A WALK ON THE WILD SIDE

THE MARTELLO TOWER, Sandycove, Dublin Bay. A seaside spot on the DART line, a kind of overground Tube train that weaves briefly into Dublin for three stops, then swerves its way out again. It's here, at this squat, fat tower that *Ulysses* begins, with Buck Mulligan descending its central stairway. The scene is almost filmic, and I wondered if the set as it were, was still intact, if the place, which lived in Joyce's memory, could be viewed and reviewed, and moved through in the same way. The tower is open to the public now as the James Joyce Museum. I noticed on my way that its address is vague: The Martello Tower, Sandycove, Dublin. No street name, no door number. No cartological reference points: I would just need to see it on the horizon, and move towards it, like in the days before there were maps.

The Martello Tower in Sandycove, as it is today

As I walked down Dublin's Pearse Street towards the DART station, I'd seen a crazy white statue which appeared to be poking up between the different roofs. Standing there, plinthless, its arms waving about. In the distance, it looked like a silhouette of a figure with splayed arms: as I approached, it whitened into a religious sculpture – a blessed saint. I realised its spread-eagled limbs were in fact criss-crossed, stumpy columns, positioned behind the figure like cannons on the diagonal. High, high up in the air, sitting between the tallest buildings, it reminded me of the opening to Fellini's *La Dolce Vita*, with the statue of Christ flying through the sky, hanging from a helicopter. Powerful but ludicrous in space. I couldn't tell which building it belonged to. I stared at it for about 100 yards as I walked down the road: it was so odd, the way it seemed perched on a wonky horizon of multifarious roofs. Pearse Street gets shabbier as you head out, with one-off, fusty shops which look closed down.

Sale of the last century? Old-fashioned window display in contemporary Dublin

Now at the DART, I am directed to a train going to Bray. The Joyce family moved here in 1887 when Joyce was five years old. Early episodes of *Portrait* are set in Bray, including the scary evocation of Joyce's governess Mrs 'Dante' Hearn Conway, a staunch Catholic and Nationalist. And the damning arguments about Parnell at Christmas dinner, where the young Stephen (and presumably Joyce) saw grown men weep for the dead politician. Bray features in Joyce's later life too, as one of the last stopping off points for his daughter Lucia before she was finally institutionalised. Her developing madness was allowed to run riot as, unsupervised, she lived in a little bungalow there, setting fire to rugs. Joyce and Nora remained in Paris, arguing over what was to be done with her, devolving responsibility to others and agonising over the consequences.

The other end of the line is Howth, and though I'm not going that way, a guide book I have suggests that the best sights outside of Dublin are to be had along this branch of the line: make sure you sit by the window facing the

The Auld Dubliner, Temple Bar

sea. Howth Head crowns the pretty town: in *Ulysses* Leopold Bloom
remembers proposing to Molly on the crag. In *Finnegans Wake*, Howth Castle
and Environs becomes the acronym HCE: signifying both the novel's main
character Humphrey Chimpden Earwicker, as well as the more universal
Here Comes Everybody. Even when condensing meaning in a complex,
associative way, Joyce preferred working with places he knew. On an
historical level, Howth is the last view nineteenth-century emigrants would
have had of Ireland. I wonder if Joyce and Nora watched it fade away behind
them, standing on the deck of the boat in 1904.

The electric trains which pass along the DART are boxier than those of the
London Underground, squared off at the front. But like the one-time trams
in this city, they are nippy and clean-running, so that in spite of the

View from Howth Head, from a late 19th-century illustration

modernity of their grinding wheels and electric hum, there is a connection to some other time. They skirt the city freely, snakily making their way over bridges. The cityscape changes quickly through the moving window. First the glassy office blocks, where business people make money. I glimpse another odd sculpture, a balletic figure crawling on its belly up the side of a dark-walled skyscraper. Suddenly a half-familiar place, recognised from the television: Landsdowne Road, home of the rugby ground, which you can see from the train. Joyce lived near here from March to August 1904. He was renting rooms at 60 Shelborne Road when he met Nora, and his first letters to her bear this address.

As the train hums on, we pass smaller Edwardian houses, before a glut of 1930s semi-detached homes, pebble-dashed and double-glazed. On the other side I see an old gasworks, its red frame faded by the weather. The buildings are thinning out, opening into old docklands: this must be Ringsend, where Joyce went walking with Nora on their first date and after. I can see the

The lighthouse at the South Wall, Bay of Dublin, late 19th-century print

connection to Joyce's address at the time, though it would have been less convenient for her, living in the city centre as she did. Then some Victorian bungalows as we move through grander outer suburbs. Gardens become more adventurous, tended by professionals. I notice more and more spiky, tropical plants, in carefully landscaped settings.

On through Sandymount, getting posher by the minute. The Georgian architecture has returned, the avenues of elegant buildings. I wonder how many of them are listed: there are so many of them after all – more than in the whole of London I would imagine. Whole towns seem to have survived: each one, a mini-Bath. Unlike London, Dublin was never bombed in the war (Ireland, like Switzerland, stayed neutral). There was no Blitz to rip apart avenues and squares, to upset the neat, architectural lines. It was here at Sandymount that Joyce noticed the beach, the ripples and ridges of the sand, with its waterlike surface. Then at Booterstown, the beach comes right up to the DART line, and I can see the damp and puddled sand up close, marshy from

Georgian doorway

where the sea must come in. A small, low wall separates the electric tracks from the damp beach: it seems a bit risky – this long metal, electric track and an ocean of water, with only a little stone barrier separating the two. As we race along what is quite literally the seafront, I imagine the high tide less than a metre away, and hope it doesn't get too high. The gulls fly in low bunches through the empty air, and, having been first in London and then the centre of Dublin, the flatness of the coast is quite shocking, the levelness of the sea.

Next stop Blackrock, and another home for the Joyce family: they lived here for a year at 23 Carysford Avenue, a dull terrace. Passing quickly through these suburbs, I am getting a sense of the multiple homes of Joyce's childhood, growing up in fly-by-night accommodation, keeping the bailiffs at bay. John Joyce, James' father, was born into wealth, but went through life mortgaging his property to make ends meet. He saw himself as a gentleman, but was really more of a full-time bon viveur, downscaling his life as he had

Fishing boats at picturesque Howth Harbour

more and more children, unwilling to work for a living while he had things left that he could sell. John Joyce hauled the family around a dozen different addresses in and around Dublin during James' childhood. Most of the time James would have been at boarding school (he went to Clongowes Wood College when he was six and a half, then later, Belvedere (scene of the terrifying Jesuit sermon in *Portrait*). Yet the holidays must have been disconcerting: coming home at Christmas and Easter to a different address, getting used to strange places over and over again.

The train sits at Blackrock for a while, and I notice that the wind must have got up: through the window, the clouds are quickly scudding, an old-fashioned streetlight planted on the ground is an earthbound reference point to the racing sky. Its lantern quivers. And the leafy trees are starting to bluster, so that everything feels a bit unsettled and jumpy. At Sandycove I alight from the train, and already it's colder, because that's what the sea air does, chills everything.

The Custom House viewed from the River Liffey, late 19th-century print

The exit is no more than a small hut, though the turnstile is modern and chrome, like at a swimming pool. Sandycove's attractions are quiet and residential: it would be a charming, if a bit bracing, place to live. I cannot see the sea or the Martello Tower from the station exit, though a brown, heritage sign indicates the way to the James Joyce Museum. I wonder if the sign has been twisted by the wind, since it points in no particular direction. I start to walk, and the streets to my left slope downwards, which I guess must be the direction of the seafront, and where I suppose, retrospectively, the sign is pointing. Down Islington Avenue, where the smart houses do in fact remind me of London's Islington, all detached, Georgian and slightly different. One is named *Martello*, so I know I must be on the right track. Another is *Middlemarch*, so that the world of literature is ever present, as well as a sense of both English and Irish preferences.

Dublin's other Martello Tower: Sandymount in the early 1900s

Islington Avenue leads down to the seafront, and after a few seconds scanning the horizon, I see the Martello Tower, far, far away. But I know there are two, and I want to make sure I get the right one. A rotund, white, speck on the shoreline confirms that I'm on the right track. I guess this must be the Art Deco house which I've seen pictured in books, the tower's twentieth-century neighbour. I start to hike along briskly.

There, in the distance, is where *Ulysses* begins. But it's not just a literary connection, I'm here because this is somewhere Joyce has been. This is my starting point, though it looks a bit blunt on the page. But at the moment there aren't any fancy interpretations. Since arriving in Dublin this is the first place I have come to, and these are my first impressions. I snap a photo of the faraway tower, but it's difficult, with the crazy wind. My fingers are cold and fumbling, and my hair keeps blowing in front of the lens, even when I flatten my fringe back with one hand. A friendly lady stops to ask if I would like her to take a picture of me, and I decline, slightly aghast, but covering it

Howth Harbour, 19th-century engraving

up with smiles. But now as I look back over what I have written, I realise that in some way this book is about me, and about my relationship to both Joyce and Dublin. Too late now, back in London, to get a photograph of myself standing there, to find the friendly lady and do the whole thing differently. There's something difficult about this writing about somewhere from a distance: not being able to go back, check things, change things, make sure of everything. And in a way, Joyce had the same problem. He wrote all of his fiction abroad, in Trieste, Paris, Zurich. Working from memory, and from a street map from 1900. He would send little cards to his Aunt Josephine in Dublin, his dead mother's sister. Those trees outside Belvedere College, were they beech trees? Would she look up the landmarks of a particular view? He was careful, thorough, plotting things in an almost military way. Scholars still catch him out though: shops in slightly the wrong position (not quite on a corner but two doors down), discovering gleefully that on the map from which Joyce worked, if something was incorrect, geographical blunders would sneak into his literature accordingly.

Dublin pub window

The Martello Tower is smaller than I had imagined: only forty foot high, with walls eight feet thick. I imagined it would be grander, bigger, like part of Windsor Castle, but here it is, surprisingly tiny. Only 200 years old, it looks almost medieval. Its design is functional, combative, built to withstand a Napoleonic invasion. The British built fifteen along the coast between Dublin and Bray: two survive. Come to think of it, I had spotted the other one on the train as I came down, and wondered whether I'd missed my stop. Just a short, blank stone turret, with no other architectural appendages. When I get closer, I can see one tiny window, near the top. And half-way up, a small barred grate.

View by the Martello Tower, looking down towards the Forty Foot

In 1904 Oliver St John Gogarty rented the Martello Tower from the Secretary of State for War, paying £8 annually. It seems to be built on an outcrop of rock, standing high. All the way along, small signs warn about large waves from passenger ferries, which can sweep on you unawares and drag you down into the sea. I can't see any passenger ferries, and the Irish Sea, notoriously choppy, looks flat and settled enough. As I walk down the path towards the tower the path narrows, splits and rejoins: take the left hand road and you can walk along a thin crag, with no railing to protect against dropping onto the rocks below. Then back along the path, which changes into a hidden alleyway between small, disused huts. It all feels slightly dangerous, a bit cloistered. I come to some steps leading back up to the safe and respectable pavement, my view of the road blocked by a skip. The steps are walled in, framing the skip neatly like a picture frame. Junky bits of rubbish are wedged into the skip, but my eye is caught particularly by a smashed red canoe, faded, scuffed and snapped in two. It's stuffed into the skip vertically, so that it pokes out above it like a candle. The canoe looks very

Those were the days: strollers on St Stephen's Green

old, and for some reason I'm drawn to it, wondering about its story. When I get back to London, I discover that Joyce and Gogarty were joined at the tower by Samuel Chevenix Trench, a friend of Gogarty's who had just returned from a canoeing trip.

A friend of mine, the writer Katherine Powlesland was intrigued by the canoe's presence, as though buildings and places continue to carry shreds of evidence which reference the past. As though there are pointers all around, you just need to start looking. It ties in with my visit to Dublin, as though following Joyce's passage through the city would somehow access the man himself. Though the literary association makes it seem more high-brow, it's still a form of tourism, this following of footsteps. And most of the time it feels quite simple: looking at buildings, taking photographs and imagining

North Earl Street, 1904

Almost at the tower now, it looms large to my left as I follow a swirling, corkscrew road which I guess will lead up to it. Climbing higher and higher over the sea, I can see why the tower was built as a look out. I hear men's voices, and I lean out over the wall. A sign says Forty Foot, and there are the gentlemen bathers, standing on rocks in their trunks. It's a bit brisk and nippy for a dip, but funny how these traditions keep going. Buck Mulligan drags Stephen Dedalus down to the Forty Foot in *Ulysses* and they see the crazy, weather-impervious swimmers. In my head, I imagined a longer walk, but here I am already at the tower's front door, just a few steps away. The tower has changed. A metal staircase used to lead up to the door on the first floor (like a fire escape). Too precarious no doubt for the general public, there is now a new entrance, though at the moment it's covered up by metal shutters, clamped down to the floor like an off license's window. It's so cold here, the wind is actually whistling, which I thought only happened in horror films. With the museum closed, this is a deserted spot, and I find myself having to lean forward into the wind to get moving again. The voices of the swimmers

A 19th-century etching of the Cross of Muredach, Monasterboice

are blown up to me as I walk back. I am now trembling with cold (is it the wind?), and just the thought of being in the water makes me spasm. I go back via a slightly different route, via Sandycove Avenue East (the route which, after being shot at, Stephen must have taken in his walk back to Dublin), but end up going along the seafront again. I pass a tree, a thin sapling with scant foliage, bordered by wire mesh. It was planted in 1982 to celebrate the Joyce centenary. But it's awful. It won't grow out here on this chilly, rocky footpath and no wonder. They should have planted lichen, nettles or some other verminous, weedy species, something which could have railed against the icy blast coming in from the sea. This tribute has ended up being a bald stump, and I wonder how you're meant to do it. How do you do a tribute? There's a bust of Mangan on St Stephen's Green, a statue of Oscar Wilde on Merrion Square. They sell books by Irish writers at the Dublin Tourism Centre, as well as reproductions of Celtic Crosses: the only place, during my entire visit, that I came across any.

Willie Pearse's sculpture of the 19th-century poet Clarence Mangan, St. Stephen's Green

There are many tributes in Dublin itself. In fact, it's safe to say that over the last twenty or so years, Dublin has carefully organised its heritage, packaging it neatly for the cultural tourist. A series of fourteen bronze pavement plaques mark Bloom's lunchtime route through the city, reminding pedestrians of Joyce's masterwork at regular intervals, passing underfoot. Plaques in fact, are everywhere. Merrion Square is particularly inundated: WB Yeats lived at number 82, Joseph Sheridan Le Fanu resided at number 70, and at 24 Merrion Street Upper, the Duke of Wellington was born. Oscar Wilde's family home commands a formidable corner site, a white walled, elaborate palazzo at odds with the clean, red brick Georgian lines. It was outside here that Joyce arranged to meet Nora on their first date: she didn't turn up.

O'Connell Street's new fountain with its statue of Anna Livia Plurabelle,
a character in *Finnegans Wake*

3

COME FLY WITH ME

WHEN NORA BARNACLE left Dublin with James Joyce on October 8 1904, she'd known him less than four months. She'd told nobody what she was going to do, neither her family in Galway nor even her employers at Finn's Hotel. Joyce was seen off at the quay by his family. Nora kept away from him until the ship had sailed, since Joyce's father didn't know he was leaving the city with a woman, unmarried. At the time, her behaviour was scandalous.

On 10 June 1904, Joyce saw Nora Barnacle walking down Nassau Street, which runs down the side of Trinity College. I find it astonishing that we can put a date to that first meeting, that private moment nearly a century ago when Joyce stopped a girl walking past. Nora worked in Finn's Hotel on Leinster Street, as a chambermaid.

Trinity College

Nora was born in March 1884 in Galway. Her father was a baker by day and a drinker by night, and her mother eventually threw him out. In later years, Nora lamented the fact that she too, had married a drinker. It was Gogarty who'd taught Joyce to drink: during most of his adolescence, Joyce had remained almost piously abstemious. The number of pubs mentioned in *Ulysses* however, bears testament to the change in Joyce's habits.

In the late nineteenth century, Galway wasn't the backwater many imagine: it had piped water and had been gaslit since 1837. But it also had tenements amongst the worst in Europe, and there were great divisions between rich and poor. Prostitution was rife. Nora's background was ordinary, but it wasn't poverty-stricken. Joyce's upbringing was more conventionally middle-class: he won scholarships and went on to University College, Dublin. Nora went to her local school and left at the age of twelve. But she could read and

Nora in the 1930s

write: it's a myth that she was illiterate, that Joyce married a peasant girl with whom he couldn't even hold a conversation. When Joyce's father heard that his son was with a girl whose surname was Barnacle, he quipped that she'd never leave him (easy to see where Joyce inherited his punning skills). In reality it appears to be the other way round. Nora was sensible, organising and refused to stand on ceremony. She was the antithesis of Sylvia Beach (the publisher of *Ulysses*) who was always terrified of Joyce. Joyce once said that he hated intellectual women anyway.

It's easy to imagine that Joyce and Nora got along fine: that the pair fit into the comfortable model of opposites attracting. But they would have screaming rows, and one or the other was always about to leave. They remained however, perversely inseparable. When Nora went into a Paris hospital in 1928 for a hysterectomy, Joyce stayed by her side, moving into a room next door and bringing all his books with him. Samuel Beckett came daily with the post, and Joyce would leave only to buy cigarettes (even though

Nora Barnacle's house in Galway

Nora was constantly yelling at him to go away). Somehow, they kept the relationship going, in spite of their differences. Nora wrote to her sister Kathleen that artists were boring. She was more interested in hats, and was sorry that Joyce didn't write nice stories. She worried about ordinary things: her hair falling out, Joyce's dress sense, what they were going to do about money. She kept all his poetry though, and knew it off by heart. She always believed he should be a singer rather than a writer, and thought his voice was lovely. In fact Joyce did have a very fine tenor voice, and at one point considered becoming a professional singer. One of Nora's great loves was opera. In Paris, she went all the time.

When they met, Joyce was starting to make his name as a writer in Dublin: he'd got to know Yeats who recognised his potential, writing to Joyce, 'You have a very delicate talent but I cannot say whether for prose or verse…' He was becoming more aloof from his friends and relations, toying with exile as the only way to develop as a writer. He was also developing an

Pub sign in Galway

imperviousness to people: Joyce wondered whether he should stick his sisters in a nunnery and have done with them. He was in the habit of borrowing money off people. As an artist, he shouldn't have to do other work (as a 'gentleman', his father shared the same belief). And if he couldn't get money then he just wouldn't eat. In a short trip to Paris at the beginning of 1903, he would write to his mother with graphic details of his hunger, starving for days, bingeing on the occasional meal, than starving again. His mother, horrified, would pawn furniture and wire him more money, repeating the pattern. He returned to Dublin in the middle of April, having received a telegram from his father which stated that his mother was dying. She died on August 13, 1903.

By 1904, aged 22, Joyce had been in love several times, but each time it was unrequited. He'd been going to prostitutes for years, something he was yet to square with his Catholic conscience. He'd finally rejected a medical career, and made a decision to become a writer. He was proud. When Nora didn't

The fish market in Galway, 19th-century illustration

turn up for their date, Joyce was mortified. He wrote her a letter, and they arranged another meeting. I've been looking at the letter Joyce wrote to Nora, and the most interesting thing about it apart from its stiff, and rather formal overtures (he requested another appointment with her) is the fact that you get a sense of how bad Joyce's eyesight was. He'd spotted another girl with auburn hair hanging around Wilde's house, but it took him some time to work out that it wasn't Nora. Joyce wasn't wearing his glasses (contrary to modern medical practice, he'd been advised that going without could well make his eyesight stronger), and it makes me wonder how many of the land-marks I've been viewing he could have looked on with clarity. By the time Joyce was in his early thirties he was near-blind.

Joyce first 'saw' Nora on Nassau Street (Brenda Maddox notes that it probably helped that Nora was a big girl). The black railings of Trinity College run down the one side of the street, and extensive building seems to be taking place in the college grounds. I could glimpse huge ditches behind

Joyce on a balcony

hoardings. But the grand iron railings remain intact, towering over me. As I walk down the road, endless buses, including sightseeing buses, crawl past. The street is filled with bus stops and bus stands, a major Dublin thoroughfare. Nassau Street changes into Leinster Street, which is very short.

Shops have changed and become other. So finding originals, places in *Ulysses* and places relevant to Joyce's biography, you need to cross-reference, hunt for door numbers, undertake some serious ordnance survey research. Finn's Hotel remains invisible, but there are some things I can get a sense of; the very close proximity to where Nora worked and where Joyce ran into her (no more than a few hundred yards, probably considerably less). And the spot arranged for their first date. Oscar Wilde's house, on the near corner of Merrion Square, is a very short walk. Nora could have reached it in a couple of minutes after leaving work. All local, all handy, giving both a sense of the small world of Dublin at the turn of the last century, but also the way we make arrangements. As I look round, Oscar Wilde's house is still the nearest

Late 19th-century etching of Trinity College

and most significant landmark in the area, the best place to meet someone. Leinster Street is just small shop fronts (would you ever arrange to meet someone outside a shop front, unless it was a department store?), and the side of Trinity College is too sprawling, an endless line of railings.

It's moments like this when I get a sense of Joyce's Dublin: understanding the relationship between buildings, measuring the distances out, seeing the logic in Joyce's arrangements and wanderings. Even when I eventually find Finn's Hotel, the pleasure is in the sense of where it is, and how it fits into the scheme of the layout of the area, rather than the building itself. It's now Jones's Newsagents, sitting at the bottom of a Georgian terrace. The words *FINN'S HOTEL* survive on the red brick wall down the side of the building, high up, hidden by as tree. The black, spindly wintry branches form a lattice over the faded writing, making it easy to miss. It's a simple, smallish, elegant building, the original sash windows still in place. Funny to think that Nora must have fiddled with these very windows, hoisting them open to air

Old signage glimpsed through a tree: the former Finn's Hotel today

rooms. It's the first building you come across where the Trinity College railings end. But up above, the buildings themselves are less altered, and the clues are still there: too high up though for the new shopkeepers to bother about. I realise that I've been looking at frontages, frustrated by the invasion of the twentieth century, the aluminium framing and security glazing. Time to start looking a different way.

Trinity College

4

HERE, THERE AND EVERYWHERE

LEAVING LONDON on my way to the airport, a blind woman got on the train. I sat down opposite her. She knew exactly when to get up for her stop, where the door was, and the distance away from the platform. I looked through the window over my shoulder, and saw her slipping through the exit easily, slotting her ticket into the machine. Her transit seemed nothing short of miraculous, but really came through concentration and a process of ongoing, steady plotting: counting distances out as she went along. I'm wondering if this ties in with Joyce's tracking of the Dublin streets. He remembered Dublin not so much as it appeared, but how it felt to move through. With such bad eyesight, he committed the skeleton of the city to memory, finding his way about through the street map in his own mind. The more I think about it, the more I'm starting to realise that there's not a lot of visual detail in Joyce's depiction of Dublin. An architectural detail outside the

Greene's bookshop

Bank of Ireland would have been invisible to him, but he would have committed to memory the curve in a street, the kink in the road where the Bank of Ireland stands, across from the main gate of Trinity College. Like the turnstile at the National Library (Stephen notices its clicking as he pushes through it in *Portrait*), he charted those things which intruded on his person, the things he could feel, in a more invasive way than the simply visual. Street furniture is of particular interest to him, postboxes, railings, as well as the texture of things (the feel of scratchy gravel when you're pushed over, as in the Clongowes episode in *Portrait*). Joyce's myopia also fits in with the way people come and go in the book: half-glimpsed, or appearing from nowhere, his characters often seem to spring up in front of his face. I'd always seen this as a nod to Dante (who used similar methods in *The Divine Comedy*). But maybe its drama comes from the constant visual surprises only the very short-sighted can experience: everything is quite literally in your face, with no sense of approach.

Architectural detail opposite the Bank of Ireland

The modernisation of Dublin causes problems for Joyce-seekers. Greene's bookshop for instance, where I sheltered from the rain under its elaborate old canopy. I wondered if this place was known to Joyce, and if so, why it slipped through his fingers, unlogged. I suppose that he couldn't reference everything – though in some sense maybe he tried. Many of the old-fashioned frontages which have survived in Dublin go unmentioned in the work, though look to the biography and they crop up here and there. When he won an exhibition grant at Belvedere College, he immediately went to Barnardo's and bought his mother a fur coat (he was generous with his money when he had it). I assumed Barnardo's to be a charity shop, so it was a delight to stumble across it, a once-upmarket furriers on the top end of Grafton Street, round the corner from the Bank of Ireland. Untouched by the twentieth century, Barnardo is written in a gilded, golden scrawl, against a lawn green background. The B of Barnardo is shaped so that it seems to swell out into the tail of a fox, and a pointed muzzle alongside completes the silhouette. I wonder how many customers they must have in these days of

Detail of gate outside Trinity College

faux fur and vegetarian chic: it looks dark inside, empty. The window display

is old-fashioned and dowdy: coats are positioned on stands rather than

mannequins, so that they seem to float in the air, headless. Others rest on

plinths so that that they trail on the floor in a becoming way. The whole thing

looks as though it's been fussily masterminded by an old lady, arranging

things carefully. On the street outside Barnardo's, a bronze civic sculpture of

Molly Malone is surrounded by sightseers. It has little aesthetic value: as with

most town centre sculpture the artist hasn't put their name to it. It's more of

a commemorative reminder of a famous citizen, and this is enough for

people to flock round taking pictures, me included.

Merrion Square. Stephen turns his face in this direction in *Portrait*, and it

often crops up in *Ulysses* as an area the characters pass through. It's

Barnardo the furriers, looking much like it did in Joyce's day

something to do with the place being so charming. But also, lying close to the city centre, its four corners provide different routes into town, different ways in to the middle of Dublin. The National Gallery of Ireland is here as well as the Natural History Museum. Towards the end of my trip I notice that I am outside the Dáil, which confuses me as I'd already seen it next door to the National Library on Kildare Street. In my mind these were different corners of Dublin, but after a bit of background reading, I discover that the Dáil has different entrances: two frontages which are connected by a long corridor. Claimed as a prototype for the White House in Washington DC, its American counterpart was designed by James Hoban, born in 1762 in Co Kilkenny. All sorts of things have their roots in Dublin, it would appear.

I'm interested in this idea of splitting buildings and multiple addresses: the way buildings can fill out onto different roads. These are all small details which Joyce would have known: the lie of the land – how it all fits together.

A contemporary view of the Dáil, viewed from Kildare Street

The city is taking shape in my mind. I seem to come back again and again to Merrion Square, as though the place is some kind of lynchpin on which the whole city hangs.

There are few gateways into Merrion Square itself, marked off as it is by black railings, and so I circumnavigate its perimeter, looking at houses. It's the road of the famous. This is the prime heritage site of Dublin, though most of these grand houses now seem to be offices: businesses can evidently afford to pay more rent than families. Once I enter the square, I am surprised by its neat landscaping, by the immaculate grooming of the lawn, which, soft and weedless, looks like a golf course. I see a mound, a man-made, artificial little hill. It reminds me of the lumps on Blackheath, where the earth was piled up after the digging of mass graves for plague victims. And I wonder if there is such a gruesome history behind that one-off lump rising out from the ground, in this green and pleasant place. Neat tarmac paths criss-cross the lovely lawn, and the bushes are pruned

The Dáil from Upper Merrion Street

carefully, into nice orbs. Hedges are cut low and straight, little knee-high borders around flower beds, trees, occasional statues. The snowdrops are out, and the daffodils. As I look across the square I get a sense of Dublin's skyscape for the first time since Sandycove, but here in the city it's punctured by the cranes, building the place over. I walk out, and as I leave, I glimpse the statue of Oscar Wilde, just visible through all the undergrowth and barrier of the railings. He's as near as he could be to his old house, just across the street. I can see his head and shoulder, and imagine he's reclining in a louche, decadent way. The statue is clearly figurative, and from here looks as though it's painted, colouring in Wilde's clothes and hair like a waxwork.

I wish I was allowed to walk down the long corridor in the Dáil: to cut through the building's secret innards to get back to Kildare Street. But I'm not, and I walk round the block the long way, back to where I was before at the National Library. It's a neat, classical building, with the flat, white,

Green and pleasant land: sculpture in Merrion Square

smooth steps, curving round its front entrance. In *Portrait*, Stephen stands on these steps, looking at the colonnade which reminds him of a temple. Inside, a complicated mosaic floor, and a library shop, which includes some souvenir-selling amongst the pencils and pens. Burly security guards let me into the reading room, after taking my bags from me and locking them up. Then, like Stephen, I go up the stairs (he didn't have to bother with all this security palaver in the first years of the twentieth century). The turnstile Joyce recorded in *Portrait* is gone, if it was ever there. But finally, I feel as though I am somewhere untouched, and complete. The world of learning is loathe to make architectural updates: think of Oxford and Cambridge.

There's nobody else just looking around like me: everyone is busy, studious, working. So I sit down quickly at a desk and take out an exercise book which I scribble on so as not to be conspicuous. It's a glorious room: horseshoe-shaped, with a massive skylight, letting in sunniness. The room is

The main gate at the National Library in the early 1900s

grand, with lashings of oak panelling. At last I am warm and comfortable, surrounded by the trimmings of academia. Each table has an old-fashioned, green-shaded desk lamp fixed to its middle, as well as a small wooden lectern, to carefully position a book. In *Portrait*, Stephen props his book on it. All the desks are identical, and inlaid with lush, dark green leather. It's very luxurious, and a bit fussy. And absolutely, crucially quiet, all heads bowed, people getting on. Cherubs skip round the cornicing, fat winged babies in plaster, chirpily abutting the jade walls. In the 1950s it was painted different shades of cream, so this is a new colour scheme, for the year 2000. It makes the place rather bright and zingy, and I wonder if this is the mood of the library which Joyce would have known (Joyce was sensitive to, and interested in colour – each chapter in *Ulysses* is said to evoke a different one).

Joyce spent a lot of time here around Christmas 1902, back from a short trip to Paris. When he returned to Paris he kept up his reading, spending his

Contemporary view of the National Library

days at the Bibliothèque Nationale, and his nights in the Bibliothèque Sainte-Geneviève. He was reading Ben Jonson and Aristotle, and brushing up on Aquinas. Towards the end of *Portrait*, Stephen's complicated aesthetic musings which he expounds to Lynch (as they leave this building), took form here in Joyce's mind. At this stage in his life Joyce treated reading as kind of full-time occupation, rehearsing the life of writer and artist. It's generally assumed that Joyce's knowledge of literature was broad, but in fact, its breadth owes much to this early cramming, and what Joyce knew of literature remained throughout his life eclectic and particular. He was very quickly too blind to be able to read properly, and much of *Ulysses* was written in large words printed in big crayon, standing by a window holding the page up to the light.

I'm sitting at desk number 40. The chairs and desk paraphernalia (lamp, lecterns etc.) have been positioned so that we all sit facing the same direction, as though we are sitting an exam. Nervously (quiet as the grave in

Joyce's fellow Irish writers. Top, George Bernard Shaw (1856-1950); Below; WB Yeats (1865-1939)

here), I flick a bakelite switch on my desk lamp and it pops on, clicking noisily. Oak shelves fitted into the panelling surround the central space, lined with hefty hardbacks. The books are all either red, blue or green, lending the walls a kind of patterned unity – a neat colour scheme. The reading material matches the sensible traditionalism of the space: no modern, brightly-coloured Collins Thesauri or Yellow Pages knocking about. I wonder what the books are then. I know that Joyce placed Cranley over near the dictionaries in *Portrait*, but I can't possible walk about and look at them without getting in trouble. I know Joyce got shushed at by the librarian. I'm not even sure if I'm allowed in here – what the rules are. Youngsters in burgundy sweatshirts must be the fetchers and carriers, and I wonder if this is the job Joyce envisaged for himself, when he wrote to the librarian requesting a job. More like he fancied being the actual librarian, with his own huge oak-panelled door, promising an endless suite of charming rooms. This is where Joyce first met Gogarty, down by that counter, as they both waited to collect their books. The girl next to me is looking at a paper entitled

Inside the National Library at the turn of the last century

'Dublin Improvement Bill', the elderly man on the other side is flicking through a very old edition of the Limerick Chronicle, with gloved hands. Serious scholars, picking at social history. When I leave, self-consciously, I visit the toilets and they're lovely, with thin, Victorian-style tiles and for some reason, plush, velveteen armchairs.

Grafton Street runs off the top of Nassau Street, the Trinity College end away from Leinster Street and Merrion Square. It's now pedestrianised, busy, full of familiar British chain stores: Warehouse, Miss Selfridge, Principles. In *Ulysses*, Leopold Bloom strolls down Grafton Street, a shopping street also in 1904: it's just that the nature of the shops has changed. Bloom glances in the window of the department store Brown Thomas, considers going in to buy Molly a pincushion for her birthday. Brown Thomas is still there. I went in, and antiquated details remain, such as the chandeliers, which hang here and there, backing up the halogen. Outside, its exterior has been redone: red canopies overhang neat, almost minimal rectangular windows, with clean

Grafton Street, 1904

black frames. The jeweller Weir & Son next door is one of the few shops left on Grafton Street with its original frontage, and provides some clue as to how Bloom, and Joyce, would have seen Brown Thomas. I am starting to notice a preponderance of gold lettering on these old shops. Weir & Son has flagpoles too, sticking out on the diagonal over Grafton Street. Flagless though. In our modern times, we don't like too much pageantry. Later, I read in a guide book that Brown Thomas has changed locations. That the former site is now home to Marks and Spencer, and that Brown Thomas was forced to cross the street. There's something quite amusing about a whole department store jumping across this thin road, years after Joyce left. Especially as Joyce no doubt took care to position it in the right place. But the shop still seems to have some original fixtures: I wonder if they took them with them, or whether the chandeliers belonged to the building they moved into, and they inherited them with the space. I am starting to realise how dangerous it is to make assumptions about places from just walking

O'Neill's public house in the 21st century

around: about what they look like, what they contain, even their position. We only see what we are given: and if it looks old enough, we assume it has always been there. I was duped for many years by the Renaissance-style fronting of Buckingham Palace: it was in fact grafted on in 1913. Would an expert be able to tell? Or would they just know?

There are however, a few safe bets. Further down Grafton Street is Bewley's Oriental Café, its elaborate mosaic facade bringing a touch of de trop olde worlde splendour to the high street banality. It's made some concessions during the twentieth century: little red canopies stating Bewley's Famous Coffee & Tea (self-marketing which is a bit bald), and a cheap and cheerful sandwich board by the front door as an impromptu advert offering Afternoon Deals. It's quite dim inside, built over several floors with a meandering, wayward staircase, so that the coffee-seeker is deposited in various nooks and alcoves around the building. Though much of the original decor remains, the equipment is modern: refrigerated glass cabinets in the

Bewley's Oriental Café

self-service area. A James Joyce Room (maybe that's how you do a tribute) near the top of the building is empty, with no waiting staff around. Downstairs I can see waitresses, who ignore me. I'm not sure whether I'm meant to help myself or take a seat in a dark corner and hope someone wanders past. The most Edwardian thing about it is the vagueness of its service etiquette. It's also rather dark: all polished tables and peripheral lighting in stained glass.

Bloom's walk along Grafton Street is short, but Joyce's preparation of this episode was long. He once spent a whole day working on just two sentences, shuffling the order of the words. These days the street is slabbed in little bricks. Joyce knew it as a wooden thoroughfare, paved with hexagonal wooden blocks which could be lifted out when repairs were needed. Though Grafton Street is car-free, it opens out at the bottom into a huge gyratory system for the traffic: it's only later that I realise that I'm on St Stephen's Green. Off to the right is the Gaiety theatre, which gets a passing reference in 'The Dead', discussing the merits of a new soprano who's come to town.

Cunningham's coffee house

Now a regular venue for Opera Ireland, the musical connection is still strong. And the building itself looks more or less untouched since the nineteenth century. *Gaiety* in ritzy red writing, glows pinprick sharp on this dim and rainy afternoon. The building's facade is quite shabby, which I like.

Stephen's Green (Dubliners, Joyce included, drop the 'St') is walled, with a grand, classical entrance (a bit like London's Marble Arch). I'd expected something smaller, quainter, not this grand, Palladian border. Once inside the traffic noise makes the place seem a bit dingy. The lake and ducks are charming, but crammed with people as it is, it seems an unlikely place for a quiet moment now. A few drunks wander around, and the passers-by walk briskly, using the Green as a cut-through, rather than as a place to meander and enjoy. Barely through the gate and it starts raining. So I left, with little incentive to go back. Stephen's Green was one of Joyce's favourite places in the city.

Contemporary photograph of the Fusilier's Arch, St Stephen's Green

And then the seedier side of town, a twenty minute walk away. Mabbot Street is no longer, renamed Corporation Street. Leopold Bloom wanders up here in *Ulysses*, where it's a road of prostitutes, debauchery, noise. Different dogs seem to tail Bloom (Joyce's worst nightmare – throughout his life he was as terrified of dogs as he was of thunder). It's still a residential area, but I'm glad I'm on a bus. It feels a bit rough. Most of the streets have in fact been renamed, as though that changes things, takes away past notoriety, and (as Ezra Pound might say) makes it new. We pass a store for Olhausen's butchers, and I wonder if this is where they do their killing and chopping, or if this is just where the animals arrive, newly-dead. Nice to see the area has retained a certain kind of viscerality. Even the road is too narrow, causing the bus tyres to squeeze and scrape against the kerb. Then the road opens out and the housing estates begin. These are all twentieth-century, bright and fairly low-built, set back from the road. Corporation housing in Corporation Road. Mecklenburgh Street (once notorious) has been rechristened Railway Street by the council. I get the feeling the area is definitely trying to move away from its scandalous heritage, by being as deadpan and practical as possible. The area still feels poor though, and it's interesting that even after

A quiet moment in St Stephen's Green

100 years, and with massive rebuilding, the poverty of this area is little altered. The tenements may be gone, but the have-nots still wind up living on the same road. A New Ager would say it was to do with ley lines, or bad feng shui.

Still on the bus I see Mountjoy Square, round the corner from Fitzgibbon Street where the Joyces lived (another address – didn't realise that this one was quite so near the red light district in his schooldays: handy for Joyce's night-time jaunts in his teenage years). I grab a picture through the bus door, glimpse a simple Georgian terraced square. It's less ornate than Merrion Square and looks a bit scruffy, but now I'm wondering if that's because it was a rainy day, and because the bus moved through it quickly. I had no time to walk around, savour its delicacies. It's slightly dangerous that Dublin is a foreign city to me: my responses being as they are based on first impressions, on the way things look in the broad sweep of a cursory glance. Still on the bus I glimpse Fitzgibbon Street, a quick flash of a quiet, residential road.

View of Dublin in the mid 19th century

Though the bus is moving I snap a picture of it, so that thinking back, I didn't really get to see it, obscuring my view by bringing the camera up to my face. I know beforehand though that number 14 has been demolished anyway, so it's not as if now, there is anything much to see. The house is gone, the street remains. I get a flash of confusion as to what I'm meant to be looking for. Is the street on its own enough? Looking at the blurred photograph of the street now, it somehow sums up the Joyce trail, how many of these routes I'm following are changed. The roads remain, like a kind of skeleton, but the flesh on the bones – the buildings – are decomposing slowly. Further on, suiting my morbid turn of thought, I pass the Glasnevin Cemetery. Leopold Bloom walks all the way here in *Ulysses* in a funeral procession, musing on the dead. And Joyce's parents are buried here, across the way from Parnell.

Parnell's funeral in 1891, passing the old Parliament Building in College Green

Sacred Heart
of Jesus
I place my trust
in Thee

5

HOLDING OUT FOR A HERO

Parnell was part of Joyce's life and literature, even though he had died before Joyce was ten years old. Charles Stewart Parnell (1846-91), an Irish politician, entered parliament in 1875 and soon became prominent in the Irish Home Rule party. He organised a policy of obstruction, and securing the support of the Fenians, eventually became president of the Land League, an organisation set to secure the rights of tenants against the wealthy landowners (Parnell was himself a wealthy Protestant landlord). In the autumn of 1881 (six months before Joyce was born) he was imprisoned in Kilmainham Gaol for inciting violence, but he was released the following May when Gladstone intervened with the 'Kilmainham Treaty', which granted some rights to the tenants. It was an important concession by the English Government and Parnell understood this, but he continued to pressurise Gladstone on the whole issue of Home Rule. The English

The Sacred Heart of Jesus, O'Connell Street

establishment started to fight back, not so much in the Commons, but conducting what these days might be known as a smear campaign.

The Times accused Parnell of being actively involved in the crimes perpetrated by the Land League, including a vicious stabbing in Dublin's Phoenix Park of Lord Frederick Cavendish, Chief Secretary for Ireland and Gladstone's nephew. It was ultimately proved however that the documents which The Times relied on as evidence were false. But the final undoing of Parnell was the revelation that he was having an affair with Katharine (Kitty) O'Shea, a married woman. The revelations in the Press made Parnell a laughing stock, as a maid testified in court to Parnell's farcical tactics to avoid being caught by Kitty's husband, which included climbing onto balconies and down fire escapes. Gladstone stated publicly that it was impossible for Parnell to remain leader of the Irish party, and indeed, he was quickly deserted by its majority, largely due to the influence of the Catholic Church. Even though he married Kitty O'Shea, he was still perceived as an adulterer,

The power of the cross: the Catholic Church contributed to Parnell's downfall

Left, Charles Parnell; Above, Kitty O'Shea

and unfit to lead. His health deteriorated. Crippled by rheumatism and suffering from kidney disease, Parnell died less than a year later, aged only 45. When I leave my hotel on my first morning in Dublin, the first thing I see after Gogarty's house is the Parnell monument, standing at the northern end of O'Connell Street. Joyce would have known O'Connell Street as Sackville Street. It actually began life in 1700 as Drogheda Street, but was later renamed Gardiner's Mall. In a sense, Dublin has always been changing: like its political status, its landmarks and reference points have been temporary, shifting. The Parnell monument would have been unfamiliar to Joyce: it was erected in 1911, seven years after his departure from Dublin.

I remember reading somewhere that O'Connell Street is the widest street in Europe, built as a big grand avenue. It's the backbone to the city, peppered with statues, leading straight to the Liffey. It reminds me of the Champs Elysées: its width does make it striking, with the other side of the road so very far away. Part of the way down, there is an island in the middle of the

Sackville Street, 1904. Renamed O'Connell Street in the 1920s

road (mentioned in *Ulysses*) which you can wander along. Dirty light bulbs are strung and knotted around the branches of the trees, no doubt to light up the place at night and make it into a fairy tale. By day, O'Connell Street is a mess, the trams gone in favour of double-decker buses, the traffic filling both sides of the street, bumper to bumper. It smells of chip fat and exhaust fumes, and the shops are appalling: fast food places and amusement arcades. A rickety Art Deco cinema is being squatted by a man selling different types of bag. This is the sort of place where school children play truant, smoking nervously on street corners. And Parnell presides over all, in blackened bronze, standing at the bottom of a long pillar supporting what looks like a flaming torch, like the symbol for the Olympic Games.

I find it interesting that Parnell's statue is dwarfed by another structure: unlike Nelson's Column in London, where Nelson stands high on the pillar, Parnell is low to the ground, overlooked. But in a sense it fits in with Parnell as a kind of fallen hero: that even as the monument was raised, its figurehead

Memorial to Parnell

was being brought down to earth, grounded. The more I think about it, the more I find it bizarre, building this huge column then putting Parnell's statue at the bottom of it. As a commemoration, it's a bit back-handed. The analogy to Nelson's Column is especially appropriate, as it was a monument which Joyce would have known. The Dublin version of the London monument stood on O'Connell Street until 1966, when it was blown up by persons unknown. Stephen stands beneath the column in *Ulysses*, making up stories about it to his companions.

Towards the bottom of the road is the GPO, where Joyce would come to post his late-night letters to Nora (Dublin in the 1900s would have five deliveries a day. Both Joyce and Nora would often post letters at lunchtime, arranging where they would meet the same evening). In 1904, the GPO was still an innocent, functional building, a post office which, though verging on the grand side, as yet had no part in history.

Lighting on O'Connell Bridge

The Irish Volunteers and the Irish Citizen Army, who took part in the Rising, had never been taken seriously by the British authorities. They had previously been allowed to march with arms through Dublin, since it was thought better to treat them as a kind of militant joke than to engage with them, disarm them, and run the risk of turning them into martyrs. The political reason for this was that the Liberal British government was in the process of passing devolution through Parliament. In 1914, the Act had been signed by the King, and placed on the statute book, to come into force at the end of twelve months or at the end of the First World War, whichever was the longer period. In this way, the seizing of the GPO, surprised even the Irish people. After taking the GPO (largely by asking the bemused general public going about their postal business to leave), Padraig Pearse stood in front of the building and declared Ireland a republic. 'In the name of God,' ran the Proclamation 'and of the dead generations from which she receives her old tradition of nationhood, Ireland through us summons her children to her flag and strikes for her freedom.'

The General Post Office

Given that the political machinations were already underway to grant Ireland her freedom, Pearse's gesture, doomed to fail as it was, was largely symbolic. But Pearse understood that nation-building comes through symbolic actions: that war can be waged on the raising of a flag (the British did it as recently as 1982, in the Falkland Islands). The executions by the British authorities which followed the Rising turned the tide of public opinion. There were 77 death sentences, and though most would be commuted, the Irish people waited with dread to see how many were carried out. One Irishwoman wrote: 'It was like watching a stream of blood coming from under a closed door.' Padraig Pearse and his brother Willie were shot, as was the old Fenian Tom Clarke; and Thomas MacDonagh, a poet and one of the rebel commandants. James Connolly was the last, shot sitting in a chair because his ankle had been wounded and he couldn't stand up. Pearse had earlier spoken of the need for a blood sacrifice for Ireland to purify herself, and the allusion to Christ's Passion is borne out by the fact that the 1916 Rising took place on Easter Monday.

Dublin Castle

Joyce followed these events from Switzerland, choosing a neutral place to remain in exile during the war. Ellmann states in his biography that Joyce evaluated the Rising as useless. Joyce had known Padraig Pearse at University College, as a teacher of the Irish language. Joyce stopped studying Irish however due to Pearse's denigration of English. Ellmann claims that Joyce felt 'out of things', and his relationship with Ireland seems to have been becoming more complex. When asked if he would not welcome the emergence of an independent country, he claimed that his response would be to declare himself its first enemy. He declined an invitation from a magazine to write an article on Irish events. Joyce's war with Ireland was an entirely private one; in exile he nursed personal griefs. In a letter to Nora in 1904, he wrote of his battle with Ireland's religious and social forces. Unlike his father, Joyce had no interest in taking on Ireland's problems: on the contrary, he kept his distance, taking his cue from Icarus rather than Yeats, and seeking to soar up over its mire rather than become embroiled.

End of an era: Edward VII with Queen Alexandra opening his first parliament in 1901. Edward was on the throne until his death in 1910

I've been looking at a photograph of the gutted interior of the GPO following the Rising. Rebuilt in the 1920s, the inside now is beautiful, a large marble atrium, with scattered, fancy bureaux where you can stand and address letters. Norman Teeling's 1996 painting series adorns the wall like The Passion in a church, so that again, religion and nationalism seem closely linked. The GPO retains its functional elegance, with a serpentine sweep of carved, wooden counters sweeping around one side of the atrium. The rest is empty save for the little desks on which to write addresses and stick on stamps, and the post boxes, which being rather angular, have an Art Deco feel – a hint that when the rebuilding took place in the 1920s, more modern details crept in. A tramp totters up to me and warbles something, but is bustled away by the security guards. A few Japanese tourists mill about, clearly unimpressed, and not quite sure what they're looking for. A friend of mine said that the GPO was riddled with bullet holes, but inside, everything is nicely plastered and immaculate. Outside, I could see a few chips in the dirty stone, though on the whole, I couldn't tell if this was from gunfire or

William Gladstone (1809-98) was four times Prime Minister of Great Britain. A Liberal, his bill for Irish Home Rule split his own party in 1886 but he persevered, and was defeated in the House of Lords. An eloquent supporter of Irish issues, Gladstone was described by Disraeli as 'inebriated by the exuberance of his own verbosity.'

the general wear and tear of an eighteenth-century building. It strikes me now as morbid to be looking for such vestiges of violence, but in a way, it's a way of recreating in one's own mind the sense of why this place is important, a tangible reminder of events in the past. Every time I drive past Cleopatra's Needle on London's Embankment, I see the damage at the base of the sphinx, where a bomb dropped nearby in the Second World War. These places are in some sense casualties, displaying their injuries to the world as evidence that something traumatic once happened. Like ghosts, they are evidence of suffering, yet are still standing, having survived. Maybe this is what makes them appealing, objects of value. Joyce wouldn't have been keen, I imagine, on this romanticisation of places, even as I rested my fingers on the dents and crevices outside the GPO. Further down the street, is a statue of O'Connell, the Liberator. He stands on a plinth (unlike Parnell at the other end), and is surrounded by four victories. One of the victories has a bullet hole right through its nipple, but I wasn't going to climb up the three short steps and stick my finger in there.

A section of Dublin Castle, extended in the 1800s

I am also becoming interested in Oliver St John Gogarty, the model for Buck Mulligan. Coming across his house on my first morning here, the plaque on the wall describes him as a surgeon and a man of letters, putting him in the context of his own life rather than as a person Joyce knew. Later, walking past the Shelborne Hotel on St Stephen's Green, I came across another plaque, which states that this is where Gogarty kept rooms. There's a statue of Joyce on the Green, and it's bizarre that these one-time friends and contemporaries should be commemorated within a few hundred yards of one another.

The Martello Tower had already struck me as a wild, crazy place to live (Joyce preferred the sedate, rural atmosphere of Stephen's Green). The more I read about Gogarty, the more fascinating he appeared. Already a senator in the Civil War of 1922, Gogarty was abducted by Republicans and escaped by swimming the Liffey whilst under fire. He cuts a very different figure to Joyce, who feared violence so much he couldn't even bear to put a fight in

Ardilaun Lodge, St Stephen's Green

Ulysses. Whilst being shot at in the Liffey, Gogarty promised the river that if he survived, he would release swans on it. He lived, and he did. One afternoon as I fumbled with a map, a man called Ken offered to walk me to my hotel, telling me I was going in the wrong direction, and that I was heading down towards Portobello. 'Is that where the canal is?' I asked, and he nodded. 'Are there swans on the canal?' I asked. 'Yes, that's right,' Ken said blankly and I thought, 'Gogarty's swans,' and almost swooned.

Joyce and Gogarty fell out, the last straw for Joyce was the shooting incident at the Martello Tower. And in a way, writing about Joyce I expect to take his side, but finding Gogarty rather seductive complicates the issue. When I wrote a book on Wordsworth, I found myself becoming more interested in Coleridge, another pair of friends who had their differences. And it does make it difficult, because in a sense, you do need some kind of love for the person you're writing about, or the book becomes malicious, a hatchet job. When Joyce returned to Dublin in 1909 he blanked Gogarty in Merrion

Dublin as it was planned in the late 18th century.
Top; Sackville Street, (O'Connell Street.); Below; the Royal Exchange

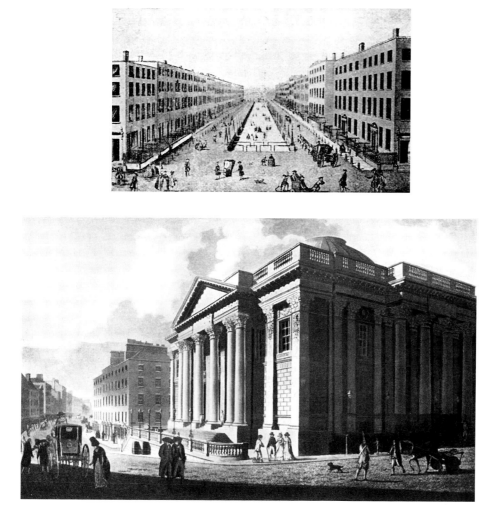

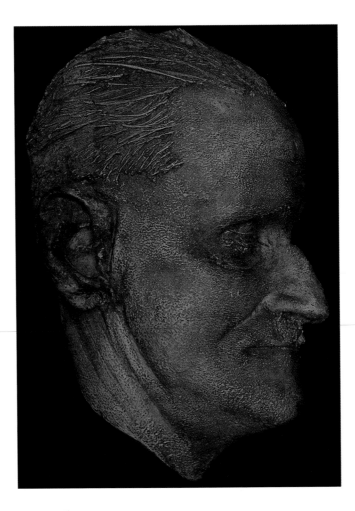

Square. Even just reading about it, upset me. It was as though I took it personally, having somehow decided that I liked Gogarty, I couldn't understand why Joyce was being so difficult about him. Gogarty actually ran after Joyce, took his arm and insisted he come round to his house. Joyce went, but felt Gogarty just wanted to show off how rich he had become. Joyce remained aloof, refusing to sit down and take a drink and offering veiled warnings of his intended portrayal of Gogarty in literature. The breach seemed irrevocable. It's curious though that on the day Joyce died he had only two books on his desk: a Greek Lexicon and Gogarty's *I Follow Saint Patrick*.

Too little information is a dangerous thing: trying to process snatches of gossip about people you don't know. It's terrifying, how quick we are to judge. More background reading, and I start to realise that Gogarty doesn't seem like a very nice person at all. Apparently he described Joyce's declining, long-suffering mother as a 'naked nerve'. And even after Joyce's death, he

Joyce's death mask

continued to pick at his skeletons in the closet. He would pass on reports from the ghouls who went to see Joyce's daughter Lucia in the mental hospital, laughing about how she dreamed of marrying, when 'she is grey haired and has a little beard.' So maybe Joyce was right to blank him in the street, convinced as he was of Gogarty's core nastiness. It's impossible to get to the bottom of these things. It's also rather shocking to think that many of Lucia's visitors were Joyce scholars, going to see her right up until her death in 1982.

How do you measure the life of a writer? Even Richard Ellmann's scholarly biography of Joyce, considered one of the greatest biographies of the twentieth century, has in recent years had some serious accusations levelled at it. Joyce's brother Stanislaus emerges as a near martyr in it and Joyce, self-centred and indifferent. It's emerged that Stanislaus had a huge cache of letters, diaries and papers, some of which Joyce left with him to look after. And recent researchers have discovered that some letters, which they know

The Dublin Writers' Museum

were written, are not included in the collection. It's now thought that Stanislaus edited his archive, culling anything which did not show him in a good light. Stanislaus' papers were the major source of reference for the Ellmann book, and if the book reveals a very skewed picture of the relationship between the two brothers, it might well be because the one left alive at the end decided to manipulate the evidence.

View of the Law Courts by the Liffey, late 19th century

6

TAKE A CHANCE ON ME

I'M SITTING IN a bar near the Custom House desperately searching for some evidence to manipulate, having yet another coffee. I'm tired because I didn't sleep last night. There was a rock concert, believe it or not, at my hotel. All these things we have to contend with: eating and sleeping and rock concerts – all the invisible things, uncharted, hiding behind the crisp and ordered type on the page. When what I need is sex and lies and family hysterics, *Hello!* magazine-style gossip to pepper my book with, make it all saucy and readable and fun. But I know that I don't want to go down that road. It strikes me however, that the parameters for this book are quite limited: looking at landmarks and matching them with events in Joyce's life and literature. Spotting things and ticking them off my list, in a sporadic,

Relief at Dublin Castle

efficient way. I feel like I need more, and this is where writers get onto dangerous ground, changing the brief to include riskier things.

I decide to do a Joyce walk, to follow in the footsteps of Leopold Bloom. I need some structure, and who better to give it to me than Mr Joyce himself. What is *Ulysses* if not a day long walk through the city? Answer: it's not. Different characters head off in different directions, and the distance covered is no stroll. Bloom coves about eight miles on foot and a further ten by tram, train and horse-drawn vehicle. Stephen covers nearly ten miles just to get back to Dublin from the Martello Tower.

I have Robert Nicholson's *Ulysses Guide* with me however, offering 'Tours Through Joyce's Dublin'. I get my bearings peering through the coffee shop window (it's cold out, I'm sure I could get more done in the summer). I see a large building in the style of Buckingham Palace, topped by a green dome in the manner of St Paul's Cathedral. I've been spotting this dome all over

Some walks have more structure than others: Dollymount

Dublin, popping up in front and behind me all over the city, and I've never yet been able to set my bearings by it. Even today after extensive walking about, north, south, east and west are foreign to me, and I get lost easily. But now that I have established that this building is the Custom House, I'm sure all that's going to change. (Later tonight I look out of my hotel window and see on the horizon, the green dome of the Custom House. What on earth is it doing over there? It's done a Brown Thomas on me, and moved to a different location. It must be a different green dome, another building tricking my eye. No wonder I keep getting lost.)

Sitting here in this coffee bar by Tara Street Station, I'm at a crossroads. According to Nicholson, there are several walks I could choose. Nicholson has followed Joyce's example, and labelled his walks according to chapters in *Ulysses*, and here, where I sit, different paths in the book criss-cross: *Eumaeus*, *Lotuseaters*, *Wandering Rocks*. Wondering which route I should take, I look up some of the landmarks along the granite quays, to see if any of them

The Custom House

take my fancy. Today my mood is lackadaisical, disordered, random. The Ha'penny Bridge, Courts of Justice and further along, the Guinness Brewery. Guinness remains one of Dublin's major exports. Adverts abound around the city, and across the road from the O'Connell monument, a 1970s skyscraper has the name of the brand descending its side wall, in slightly kitsch lettering. I wonder if this tower block is their head office. It might be nice to go to the brewery and have a pint of Guinness – that would be the authentic Dublin experience. As I bite into my biscuit I notice its brand rising up out of its crust: Lotus. I am flabbergasted, quite literally by the hand that feeds. I am a Lotuseater. The Lotuseater chapter it is then. My decision has been made for me, hand-picked by the gods. I wonder if Joyce would approve of my serendipitous approach to exploring his city, and decide that, despite his rationalist posturing, he was as superstitious as they come. Joyce was interested in séances, and wondered if his daughter Lucia was clairvoyant.

Ha'penny Bridge

My walk turns out to be awful, which just goes to show how mean-spirited Fate can be. I should have probably been more sensible about it, warned by Nicholson's description of it as 'Bloom's unnecessarily circuitous route from home'. Bloom walks along Sir John Rogerson's quay. The area seems in a process of renovation, the quay itself having been spruced up sometime probably in the 1980s. The pavement seems widened on the waterfront side, and there are litter bins and baby trees, setting the scene for what might be a more pleasant walk in fifty or so years. But the shops away from the water remain quite ramshackle, with haulage site offices and ironmongers, a reminder that in the past, this was an area for working men. After a bit I don't see anyone, though the traffic is still heavy and again, as always in Dublin, it's impossible to cross the road. Following Bloom's route I turn right into Lime Street, passing a modern brick office block. The street is still deserted. Then right again down Townsend Street, so that I am doubling back in the direction I came, walking parallel to the quay but back the other way. Townsend Street is a mix of the old and new: with concrete-fronted council

Eden Quay, 1897

housing stretching all the way down the left hand side. I realise that not only am I walking in circles, that this could well be one very dodgy street (how do I know?) and there is absolutely no one else around. It's the quietness of the area that doesn't inspire confidence, the fact that though it's the middle of the afternoon, I don't see a single other person. I can't believe that I walked straight into this based on what was written on my biscuit. It's a no-win situation. Now that I'm away from the big grand buildings of the city centre, I long for the crowds, handicams and carefully charted cultural tourism, the safety of numbers and being on a fixed path. I consider heading back and boarding a sightseeing bus: a glimpse of Dublin Castle and St Patrick's Cathedral suddenly seems like the most fascinating thing in the world.

My walk was far from a leisurely, sightseeing stroll, more of a slightly panicked rush through a dodgy area of the docks, keeping my camera well under wraps. The circularity of my route is also quite hilarious. Backwards and forwards, Bloom is meandering about, heading nowhere in particular

Dublin Castle

and I'm following him. This is one of the strolls where the walker is out to get a breath of air, thinking private thoughts, passing through space. But I'm here to see things, to soak it all up, but here there's not really anything to see as such. I miss my turning and come out onto a huge one-way system, and decide I may as well make my way back towards the centre of town. Back onto Pearse Street, which will take me back in, I stupidly walk down it the wrong way so that I'm back at the DART, where I was this morning on the way to the Martello Tower. I have been walking all day, and have come back to my starting point. There is the crazy statue again, guns blazing high in the sky. I follow it to its front door out of interest, and discover that it's St Andrew's Church. Renamed 'All Hallows' in *Ulysses*, Bloom pops in, to sit quietly in a corner. It's funny that I should cover such a ludicrous amount of mileage, missing this prime location first time round, even after pondering its statue in the sky.

19th-century etching of St Patrick's Cathedral

Inside, the church appears untouched, though I'm learning now that first impressions can be deceptive. The light is soft and peach-coloured, for some reason. Far away, I hear a phone ringing. It sounds old-fashioned, a bell rather than a beep, making a din. No-one's answering, and I wonder if now, here today, God is at home. Women come and go, kneeling and praying, lighting candles. I notice the confessionals, three on each side-wall. Each little oak-carved cabin is very thin, protruding less than a couple of feet into the space. These little rooms must be built into the very walls of the place itself, descending deep into the sides of the building, like air raid shelters. They have dark red velvety curtains, super-textured, like flock wallpaper. Last night I read how chintz has a shiny surface which dust slides off, hence its popularity in the home. But these curtains are thick and heavy, soaking up the whispers of sinners, and also in some sense, soaking up time itself. When I came in, I genuflected out of habit. Though I've stopped going to church, years of childhood mass still produce certain god-fearing reflexes, and a

Statue of Mary outside a Dublin church

fundamental, slightly superstitious awe of churches. I make a donation, light a candle and pray quietly before leaving. Glancing up from where I'm kneeling, I suddenly realise that the figure of Joseph has been positioned so that he appears to be looking at me. It's disturbing to finish prayer, look upwards and catch his painted eyes. They are pitiful, and full of love, yet I've never experienced such direct contact with a religious icon: the way it's been arranged to stare down at me is uncomfortable, making eye-contact the way it does. It's only a small moment, but it reminds me of Joyce's discomfort with the Church, his fear of its power to touch him, his horror of his own unshakable guilt.

Back outside the church on Westland Row, I proceed, as decided, towards the city centre and come across Sweny's chemist in Lincoln Place. As Bloom noticed in the Dublin of 1904, chemists almost never change location, and

Contemporary Dublin street

here is Sweny's, still here even now. It's still got its original name-plate and shop-front, though updated now with the gaudy neon of an advert for prescriptions, and big, modern brands: Benylin and Centrum 'Complete from A to Zinc'. I go in, and the interior is untouched. Like Bewley's, it's dark but also tiny: there's a small space for the customer to stand in the middle, surrounded by hefty wooden counters on all sides. And like Bloom, I buy some lemon soap from an elderly lady in a white coat, who wraps it carefully. Three lemon soaps cost £6.95, a present for my boyfriend which does make him smile. Since I left the Custom House I've been walking for nearly three hours (and covered only a tiny portion of *Ulysses*). It feels like 100 years.

The Custom House in the 19th century

7

STARTING OVER

When 7 Eccles St, Bloom's house, was demolished in 1982, its contents were distributed around various sites. Its front door is in Bailey's restaurant, off Grafton Street, a literary relic. I'm wondering now whether the demolition of no 7 would be allowed: in the last years of the twentieth century, Dublin started to champion Joyce as a famous former resident, reclaiming him as his own. Maybe one day they'll demolish the hospital and rebuild number 7: it could well end up being recreated on its former site, like Shakespeare's Globe Theatre.

In 1962, the James Joyce Museum was opened at the Martello Tower, by Sylvia Beach. Funny to think she was still alive then: she seems to be part of a much earlier time. She makes me think of Gertrude Stein, Freud and Joyce himself, middle-aged already when the *Titanic* sank, all of whom were dead

The lake in St Stephen's Green

before the Second World War was out. Beach was one of the stragglers, like Picasso or Dali, making it through to more modern times. Or Marcel Duchamp, who had his photograph taken with Andy Warhol.

It's curious this notion of celebrity. The idea of the Joyce scholars visiting Lucia has upset me, going to see a mad old lady in a mental hospital, after Joyce had been dead forty years. It's because people seek connections. I remember meeting Merlin Holland, Oscar Wilde's grandchild, running into him on the street somewhere in London. I didn't realise who it was until someone pointed it out after he'd gone. I heard someone refer to him as 'the blood royal', and there is some kind of need to stay connected, to find a way back to the individuals themselves.

For me, the blood line was coming to Dublin. But as I look back over the book I have written, I realise that it doesn't fit any particular model. It's

Joyce and Sylvia Beach

neither a travel book, a biography, nor an examination of Joyce's literature. Dublin floats about somewhere in its middle, a series of impressions built into a meandering, wayward narrative. But this was the Dublin I encountered, and the Dublin I remembered. What I have recorded is that sense you take away when you leave somewhere, a series of imprecise, cloudy recollections which float in the memory. I know that other books are more exact than mine. And I could have used my Cambridge education to gather up facts, cramming them in to offer you all the information in the world. But I was more interested in the blue clock on the front of Trinity College, glowing bright in the sunshine after a warm shower of rain. And I think, as Joyce got older, that one of the reasons he wouldn't go back was that he didn't want to damage his impressionistic view of the city. Like Monet, what Joyce sees seems to emerge from the written equivalent of little dabs: buildings described here and there, streets alluded to, landmarks mentioned. Joyce's Dublin is a city of fragments. And though scholars believe it can be reassembled, we shouldn't forget that that's how Joyce presented it: in bits and pieces.

Contemporary view of Trinity College

Back in London, I visit an exhibition of manuscripts and first editions at the British Library. Entitled *Chapter and Verse*, the show includes a Sylvia Plath poem which she wrote out neatly in her schoolgirl writing, with a jaunty daisy drawn on the bottom of the page. Virginia Woolf's suicide notes (ever the careful writer, she did several versions until she was happy with it) were considered too harrowing to be included. And there is a first edition of Ulysses, the book the English banned. As I look at this first edition of *Ulysses* in its glass case, I realise what I knew before even going to Dublin: that what I'm looking for is all there, and nowhere else.

The Liffey

CHRONOLOGY OF JOYCE'S LIFE

1882 James Augustine Joyce, first child of John Stanislaus Joyce

and Mary Jane Joyce (née Murray), born 2 February, in Rathgar, a

suburb of Dublin.

1884 Nora Barnacle, Joyce's wife, is born in Galway. Birth of Stanislaus

Joyce, one of nine surviving siblings, who was the closest to James.

He would later follow Joyce to Trieste.

1888 The Joyce family moves to Bray, a town in the south of Dublin.

James attends Clongowes Wood College, an élite Jesuit school. The

downfall of Parnell makes a strong impression on James.

1891 Financial difficulties force James to be withdrawn from the

college and break with his schooling.

1892 The Joyce family moves to Blackrock, a suburb of Dublin.

1893 Further financial decline and the family move to a series of

central Dublin addresses. James receives a scholarship to attend

Belvedere College, another Jesuit school.

1896   Becomes prefect of the Sodality of the Blessed

Virgin Mary which brings religious duties, but questions

increasingly his Catholic faith.

1897   Wins academic prizes, including a prize for the best English

composition in Ireland in his grade.

1898   Starts at University College, Dublin.

1899   Attends the opening night of Yeats' *The Countess of Cathleen*.

1900   Publishes articles on Ibsen in the *Fortnightly Review*, receives thanks

from Ibsen. Reads paper on 'Drama and Life' to the Literary and

Historical Society. Writes poems and plays, mostly destroyed. Death

of Oscar Wilde in Paris.

1901   Writes *The Day of the Rabblement*, which is refused by college

magazine. Joyce publishes it privately.

1902   Graduates from University College; leaves Dublin for Paris,

ostensibly to study medicine.

1903   Returns to Dublin in April on receiving news of his mother's

illness. She dies on 13 August.

Oscar Wilde c.1891

1904   Leaves the family home for a variety of residences, including the Martello Tower at Sandycove. Writes an essay entitled 'A Portrait of the Artist', and poems and stories for magazine publication (later to be included in *Chamber Music* and *Dubliners*). Starts work on *Stephen Hero*. Meets Nora Barnacle on 10 June, and leaves Dublin for the Continent with her on 8 October, unmarried. Obtains job with the Berlitz School in Pola, which was then under Austrian rule.

1905   Moves to the Berlitz School in Trieste. Son Giorgio born on 27 July. Submits *Chamber Music* and *Dubliners* to London publishers Grant Richards. Stanislaus comes to Trieste to join the family.

1906   Moves to Rome and works as a bank clerk. He writes two more stories for *Dubliners*.

1907   Returns to Trieste. His daughter Lucia is born on 26 July. *Chamber Music* is published in London He finishes the last story 'The Dead' for the *Dubliners*. He writes newspaper articles, gives public lectures and private tuition in English.

He begins to rewrite *Stephen Hero* as *A Portrait of the Artist as a Young Man*.

North Earl Street 1904

1908   Finishes three chapters of *Portrait*.

1909   Visits Dublin twice, first to sign contact with Maunsel & Co. for

Dubliners, and then to set up a cinema. His sister Eva returns with

Joyce to live with the family in Trieste.

1912   Undertakes his last trip to Ireland. He battles with his publisher in

Dublin over censorship in *Dubliners*. His editors destroy parts of

the book because of libel fears.

1913   Befriends Ezra Pound.

1914   *Portrait* starts appearing in serial form in the *Egoist*. *Dubliners* is

finally published by Grant Richards. Joyce begins work on *Ulysses*.

World War I breaks out, and Joyce faces internment in Trieste,

which was then under Austrian rule.

1915   *Exiles* completed. Joyce and family permitted to leave Trieste for

Switzerland; they settle in Zurich.

1916   *Portrait* published in New York. Easter Uprising.

1917   Completion of three chapters of *Ulysses*. First of many eye

operations. Harriet Shaw Weaver starts supporting Joyce financially.

Statue of Grattan in front of the Old Parliament House, late Victorian etching

1918   *Exiles* published in London. *Ulysses* serialisation begins in the

Little Review. End of World War I.

1919   Return to Trieste made possible by ending of war.

1920   At Pound's suggestion, the family moves to Paris, where they will

remain for twenty years at a number of addresses. Court case

prevents the *Little Review* from continuing to serialise *Ulysses*.

1921   Sylvia Beach agrees to publish *Ulysses*. Anglo-Irish treaty signed

in London.

1922   *Ulysses* published in Paris by Sylvia Beach's bookshop,

Shakespeare and Company. Civil War breaks out in Ireland.

1923   Begins 'Work in Progress', eventually published as *Finnegans Wake*.

1927   *Pomes Penyeach* published by Shakespeare and Company. Extracts

from 'Work in Progress' begin to appear in print.

1930   Marriage of James Joyce and Nora Barnacle in London. Joyce's

father dies.

Interior of St Patrick's Cathedral, 19th-century etching

1932   First grandchild, Stephen James Joyce, born to Giorgio and Helen

Joyce. Lucia has a mental breakdown.

1933   The courts in the USA allow the publication of *Ulysses*. Lucia enters

a hospital in Switzerland.

1934   *Ulysses* is first published by Random Century in the USA.

1939   *Finnegans Wake* is published by Faber and Faber in the UK and

Viking in the USA. Outbreak of World War II. Ireland declares

her neutrality. WB Yeats dies.

1940   Joyce is given permission to move to neutral Switzerland from

France.

1941   Joyce is taken ill with a perforated ulcer. He dies on 13 January,

aged 58 years and is buried in Fluntern cemetery, Zurich.

1945   World War II ends.

1949   Ireland (now Eire) declares herself a republic and ceases to be a

member of the British Commonwealth.

1951   Nora dies in Zurich.

Art Center College of Design
Library
1700 Lida Street
Pasadena-CA 91103